50 French Sandwich Recipes for Home

By: Kelly Johnson

Table of Contents

- Croque Monsieur
- Croque Madame
- Jambon-Beurre
- Parisian Ham and Gruyère Baguette
- Brie and Fig Jam Baguette
- Duck Confit Sandwich
- Ratatouille Sandwich
- French Onion Soup Sandwich
- Tuna Niçoise Sandwich
- Beef Bourguignon Sandwich
- Roasted Vegetable Panini
- Chicken Provençal Sandwich
- French Dip Sandwich
- Smoked Salmon and Cream Cheese Baguette
- Alsatian Tartine
- Pork and Apple Chutney Sandwich
- Caramelized Onion and Goat Cheese Baguette
- Steak Frites Sandwich
- Quiche Lorraine Sandwich
- Lobster Roll à la Française
- Foie Gras and Fig Sandwich
- Grilled Cheese with Tomato and Basil
- Salami and Emmental Baguette
- Chicken and Tarragon Sandwich
- Ratatouille and Mozzarella Panini
- Roasted Chicken and Avocado Baguette
- Ham, Egg, and Cheese Croissant
- French Country Pâté Sandwich
- Black Truffle and Mushroom Baguette
- Baked Brie and Apple Sandwich
- Provençal Tuna Sandwich
- Roasted Tomato and Basil Panini

- Smoked Duck and Cranberry Sandwich
- Savory Herb and Goat Cheese Tartine
- Shrimp and Avocado Baguette
- Beef and Blue Cheese Sandwich
- Duck and Orange Marmalade Panini
- Spinach and Feta Croissant
- Ham and Gruyère Croissant
- French Country Ham and Pickle Sandwich
- Sweet and Spicy Sausage Baguette
- Eggplant and Mozzarella Sandwich
- Chicken and Leek Sandwich
- Grilled Portobello Mushroom Baguette
- Pâté and Pickle Baguette
- Truffle and Mushroom Croissant
- Mediterranean Veggie Baguette
- Warm Goat Cheese and Walnut Tartine
- Roast Beef and Horseradish Sandwich
- Creamy Camembert and Apple Sandwich

Croque Monsieur

Ingredients:

- 4 slices of white or sourdough bread
- 2 tbsp unsalted butter, softened
- 4 slices of ham
- 1 cup shredded Gruyère cheese (or Swiss cheese)
- 1/4 cup béchamel sauce (store-bought or homemade)

For the Béchamel Sauce (if making homemade):

- 2 tbsp unsalted butter
- 2 tbsp all-purpose flour
- 1 cup milk
- Salt and pepper to taste
- A pinch of nutmeg (optional)

Instructions:

1. **Prepare the Béchamel Sauce (if making homemade):**
   - Melt butter in a saucepan over medium heat.
   - Stir in flour and cook for about 1 minute to form a roux.
   - Gradually whisk in milk and cook, stirring constantly, until the sauce thickens (about 5 minutes).
   - Season with salt, pepper, and a pinch of nutmeg if desired. Set aside.
2. **Assemble the Sandwiches:**
   - Preheat your oven to 400°F (200°C).
   - Butter one side of each bread slice.
   - Place 2 slices of bread, buttered side down, on a baking sheet.
   - Spread a layer of béchamel sauce on each slice of bread.
   - Top with a slice of ham and a generous portion of shredded Gruyère cheese.
   - Spread more béchamel sauce on the remaining slices of bread and place them, buttered side up, on top of the sandwiches.
3. **Cook the Sandwiches:**
   - Bake in the preheated oven for about 10-15 minutes, or until the bread is golden brown and the cheese is melted and bubbly.
4. **Serve:**
   - Remove from the oven and let cool slightly before serving.

This Croque Monsieur is a delicious, cheesy French classic, perfect for a comforting meal or a special treat. Enjoy!

Croque Madame

Ingredients:

- 4 slices of white or sourdough bread
- 2 tbsp unsalted butter, softened
- 4 slices of ham
- 1 cup shredded Gruyère cheese (or Swiss cheese)
- 1/4 cup béchamel sauce (store-bought or homemade)

For the Béchamel Sauce (if making homemade):

- 2 tbsp unsalted butter
- 2 tbsp all-purpose flour
- 1 cup milk
- Salt and pepper to taste
- A pinch of nutmeg (optional)

For the Croque Madame:

- 4 eggs
- 1 tbsp olive oil or butter for frying eggs

Instructions:

1. **Prepare the Béchamel Sauce (if making homemade):**
   - Melt butter in a saucepan over medium heat.
   - Stir in flour and cook for about 1 minute to form a roux.
   - Gradually whisk in milk and cook, stirring constantly, until the sauce thickens (about 5 minutes).
   - Season with salt, pepper, and a pinch of nutmeg if desired. Set aside.
2. **Assemble the Sandwiches:**
   - Preheat your oven to 400°F (200°C).
   - Butter one side of each bread slice.
   - Place 2 slices of bread, buttered side down, on a baking sheet.
   - Spread a layer of béchamel sauce on each slice of bread.
   - Top with a slice of ham and a generous portion of shredded Gruyère cheese.
   - Spread more béchamel sauce on the remaining slices of bread and place them, buttered side up, on top of the sandwiches.
3. **Cook the Sandwiches:**
   - Bake in the preheated oven for about 10-15 minutes, or until the bread is golden brown and the cheese is melted and bubbly.
4. **Prepare the Eggs:**

- While the sandwiches are baking, heat olive oil or butter in a skillet over medium heat.
- Fry the eggs until the whites are set but the yolks are still runny, or to your preferred doneness.

5. **Serve:**
    - Remove the sandwiches from the oven.
    - Top each sandwich with a fried egg.
    - Serve immediately.

The Croque Madame is a luxurious variation of the Croque Monsieur, topped with a sunny-side-up egg for extra richness. Enjoy!

Jambon-Beurre

Ingredients:

- 1 French baguette
- 2-3 tbsp unsalted butter, softened
- 4-6 slices of high-quality ham (such as Parisian ham or any other preferred variety)
- Optional: Dijon mustard or cornichons for extra flavor

Instructions:

1. **Prepare the Baguette:**
   - Slice the baguette lengthwise, but not all the way through—leave a hinge.
2. **Butter the Baguette:**
   - Spread a generous layer of softened butter on both sides of the baguette interior.
3. **Add the Ham:**
   - Layer the ham slices evenly inside the baguette.
4. **Optional Additions:**
   - For extra flavor, spread a thin layer of Dijon mustard on one side of the baguette or add cornichons (pickles) alongside the ham.
5. **Serve:**
   - Close the baguette, cut into sections if desired, and serve immediately.

This classic French sandwich is all about high-quality ingredients and simplicity. Enjoy the rich, buttery flavor combined with the savory ham!

Parisian Ham and Gruyère Baguette

Ingredients:

- 1 French baguette
- 2-3 tbsp unsalted butter, softened
- 4-6 slices of Parisian ham or any high-quality ham
- 1 cup shredded Gruyère cheese
- 1-2 tbsp Dijon mustard (optional)
- Freshly ground black pepper (optional)
- Fresh herbs like thyme or parsley for garnish (optional)

Instructions:

1. **Preheat the Oven:**
   - Preheat your oven to 375°F (190°C).
2. **Prepare the Baguette:**
   - Slice the baguette lengthwise but not all the way through—leave a hinge.
3. **Butter the Baguette:**
   - Spread a generous layer of softened butter on both sides of the baguette interior.
4. **Add Dijon Mustard (Optional):**
   - If using, spread a thin layer of Dijon mustard on one side of the baguette.
5. **Assemble the Sandwich:**
   - Layer the ham slices evenly inside the baguette.
   - Sprinkle the shredded Gruyère cheese over the ham.
6. **Bake the Baguette:**
   - Place the assembled baguette on a baking sheet.
   - Bake in the preheated oven for 8-10 minutes, or until the cheese is melted and bubbly and the bread is golden brown.
7. **Season and Garnish (Optional):**
   - Once out of the oven, you can add freshly ground black pepper and sprinkle with fresh herbs like thyme or parsley for extra flavor.
8. **Serve:**
   - Cut the baguette into sections and serve immediately.

This Parisian Ham and Gruyère Baguette combines the richness of Gruyère cheese with the savory taste of Parisian ham, all encased in a crusty baguette. Enjoy!

Brie and Fig Jam Baguette

Ingredients:

- 1 French baguette
- 6-8 oz (170-225g) Brie cheese, sliced
- 1/4 cup fig jam
- Fresh arugula or spinach (optional)
- Freshly ground black pepper (optional)

Instructions:

1. **Prepare the Baguette:**
    - Slice the baguette lengthwise but not all the way through—leave a hinge.
2. **Assemble the Sandwich:**
    - Spread fig jam evenly on one side of the baguette.
    - Layer the Brie slices on top of the fig jam.
3. **Optional Additions:**
    - If using, add a handful of fresh arugula or spinach for a touch of greenery.
    - Season with freshly ground black pepper if desired.
4. **Serve:**
    - Close the baguette, cut into sections if desired, and serve immediately.

This Brie and Fig Jam Baguette is a delightful blend of creamy Brie and sweet fig jam, perfect for a sophisticated snack or a light meal. Enjoy!

Duck Confit Sandwich

Ingredients:

- 2 duck confit legs (store-bought or homemade)
- 4 slices of crusty bread (such as ciabatta or sourdough)
- 2 tbsp duck fat or unsalted butter, for toasting
- 1/2 cup fig jam or cranberry sauce
- 1/4 cup Dijon mustard
- 1 cup fresh arugula or spinach
- 1/4 cup thinly sliced red onions
- 1/4 cup sliced pickles (optional)

Instructions:

1. **Prepare the Duck Confit:**
   - Heat the duck confit legs in a skillet over medium heat until the meat is warmed through and the skin is crispy. Remove from heat and shred the meat from the bones, discarding the skin and bones.
2. **Toast the Bread:**
   - Heat duck fat or butter in a skillet over medium heat.
   - Toast the bread slices until golden brown on both sides.
3. **Assemble the Sandwich:**
   - Spread a layer of fig jam or cranberry sauce on one side of each bread slice.
   - Spread a layer of Dijon mustard on the other side of the bread slices.
   - Layer the shredded duck confit on one slice of bread.
   - Top with fresh arugula or spinach, red onion slices, and pickles if using.
   - Close with the remaining bread slices.
4. **Serve:**
   - Cut the sandwich in half if desired and serve immediately.

This Duck Confit Sandwich combines rich, flavorful duck with sweet fig jam and tangy mustard for a gourmet twist on a classic sandwich. Enjoy!

Ratatouille Sandwich

Ingredients:

For the Ratatouille:

- 1 eggplant, diced
- 1 zucchini, diced
- 1 red bell pepper, diced
- 1 yellow bell pepper, diced
- 1 onion, diced
- 2 cloves garlic, minced
- 1 can (14.5 oz) diced tomatoes (or 2 cups fresh tomatoes, chopped)
- 2 tbsp olive oil
- 1 tsp dried thyme
- 1 tsp dried basil
- Salt and black pepper to taste

For the Sandwich:

- 4 slices of crusty bread (such as ciabatta or sourdough)
- 4 tbsp goat cheese or ricotta cheese
- Fresh basil or parsley for garnish (optional)
- Balsamic glaze or reduction (optional)

Instructions:

1. **Prepare the Ratatouille:**
   - Heat olive oil in a large skillet or Dutch oven over medium heat.
   - Add onion and garlic, and cook until softened.
   - Add eggplant, zucchini, red bell pepper, and yellow bell pepper. Cook, stirring occasionally, until the vegetables start to soften (about 10 minutes).
   - Add the diced tomatoes, dried thyme, dried basil, salt, and black pepper. Stir to combine.
   - Reduce heat to low and simmer for 15-20 minutes, until the vegetables are tender and the flavors meld together. Adjust seasoning as needed.
2. **Prepare the Bread:**
   - While the ratatouille is simmering, toast the bread slices if desired.
3. **Assemble the Sandwich:**
   - Spread a layer of goat cheese or ricotta cheese on each slice of bread.
   - Spoon the ratatouille mixture over the cheese.
   - Garnish with fresh basil or parsley if using.
   - Drizzle with balsamic glaze or reduction if desired.
4. **Serve:**

- - Close the sandwich with another slice of bread, cut in half if desired, and serve immediately.

This Ratatouille Sandwich features a hearty and flavorful vegetable medley with creamy cheese, offering a satisfying and delicious option for lunch or a light dinner. Enjoy!

French Onion Soup Sandwich

Ingredients:

For the French Onion Soup:

- 4 large onions, thinly sliced
- 3 tbsp unsalted butter
- 1 tbsp olive oil
- 2 cloves garlic, minced
- 1 cup beef broth
- 1 cup chicken broth
- 1/2 cup dry white wine (optional)
- 1 tsp dried thyme
- 1 bay leaf
- Salt and black pepper to taste
- 1-2 tbsp all-purpose flour (optional, for thickening)

For the Sandwich:

- 4 slices of crusty bread (such as sourdough or ciabatta)
- 1 cup shredded Gruyère cheese (or Swiss cheese)
- 2 tbsp unsalted butter, softened
- Fresh thyme leaves for garnish (optional)

Instructions:

1. **Prepare the French Onion Soup:**
   - In a large pot, heat the butter and olive oil over medium heat.
   - Add the onions and cook, stirring frequently, until the onions are deeply caramelized and golden brown (about 30-40 minutes). Adjust the heat as necessary to prevent burning.
   - Add garlic and cook for another minute until fragrant.
   - Stir in the flour if using and cook for 1-2 minutes to form a roux.
   - Add the beef broth, chicken broth, white wine (if using), thyme, and bay leaf. Stir to combine.
   - Bring to a boil, then reduce heat and simmer for 15-20 minutes. Season with salt and pepper to taste. Remove the bay leaf.
2. **Prepare the Sandwich:**
   - Preheat your oven to 375°F (190°C).
   - Spread softened butter on one side of each slice of bread.
   - Place the bread slices, buttered side down, on a baking sheet.
   - Toast the bread in the oven for 5-7 minutes, until lightly golden.
3. **Assemble the Sandwich:**

        - Remove the bread from the oven and sprinkle a generous amount of shredded Gruyère cheese on one slice of each sandwich.
        - Place the other slice of bread on top to form a sandwich.
        - Return the sandwiches to the oven and bake for an additional 5-7 minutes, or until the cheese is melted and bubbly.
    4. **Serve:**
        - Slice the sandwiches in half if desired and serve hot.
        - Garnish with fresh thyme leaves if desired.

This French Onion Soup Sandwich captures the essence of the classic soup, with gooey cheese and caramelized onions enveloped in toasted bread. Enjoy!

Tuna Niçoise Sandwich

Ingredients:

- 1 baguette or ciabatta loaf
- 1 can (5 oz) tuna, drained and flaked (preferably in olive oil)
- 2 hard-boiled eggs, sliced
- 1/2 cup cherry tomatoes, halved
- 1/4 cup black olives (Kalamata or Niçoise), pitted and sliced
- 1/4 cup green beans, blanched and trimmed
- 1/4 cup red onion, thinly sliced
- 2-3 tbsp mayonnaise or Dijon mustard
- 1 tbsp capers (optional)
- Fresh basil or parsley for garnish (optional)
- Salt and freshly ground black pepper to taste

Instructions:

1. **Prepare the Bread:**
   - Slice the baguette or ciabatta loaf lengthwise.
2. **Prepare the Ingredients:**
   - If not done already, slice the hard-boiled eggs and halve the cherry tomatoes.
   - Blanch the green beans by boiling them for 2-3 minutes and then plunging them into ice water to stop cooking.
3. **Assemble the Sandwich:**
   - Spread mayonnaise or Dijon mustard on both sides of the bread.
   - Layer the flaked tuna evenly over one side of the bread.
   - Arrange the sliced hard-boiled eggs, cherry tomatoes, black olives, green beans, and red onion on top of the tuna.
   - Sprinkle capers if using and season with salt and black pepper.
4. **Garnish and Serve:**
   - Garnish with fresh basil or parsley if desired.
   - Close the sandwich with the top half of the bread, slice into sections if needed, and serve immediately.

This Tuna Niçoise Sandwich brings together the vibrant flavors of the classic Niçoise salad in a satisfying and portable sandwich. Enjoy!

Beef Bourguignon Sandwich

Ingredients:

For the Beef Bourguignon:

- 1 lb (450g) beef chuck, cut into 1-inch cubes
- 2 tbsp olive oil
- 1 onion, chopped
- 2 cloves garlic, minced
- 1 carrot, sliced
- 1 celery stalk, sliced
- 1 cup red wine
- 1 cup beef broth
- 1 tbsp tomato paste
- 1 bay leaf
- 1 tsp dried thyme
- 1 cup mushrooms, sliced
- 1 tbsp all-purpose flour (optional, for thickening)
- Salt and black pepper to taste

For the Sandwich:

- 4 slices of crusty bread (such as ciabatta or sourdough)
- 1/2 cup Dijon mustard
- 1/2 cup shredded Gruyère or Swiss cheese
- Fresh parsley for garnish (optional)

Instructions:

1. **Prepare the Beef Bourguignon:**
   - Heat olive oil in a large pot or Dutch oven over medium-high heat.
   - Brown the beef cubes in batches, removing them from the pot once browned.
   - Add the onion, garlic, carrot, and celery to the pot, and cook until softened.
   - Return the beef to the pot, then add red wine, beef broth, tomato paste, bay leaf, and thyme. Stir to combine.
   - Bring to a boil, then reduce heat and simmer for 1.5 to 2 hours, until the beef is tender.
   - Add mushrooms and cook for another 15-20 minutes.
   - If you prefer a thicker sauce, mix a tablespoon of flour with a bit of water and stir it into the pot. Cook for a few more minutes until thickened.
   - Season with salt and black pepper to taste. Remove the bay leaf.
2. **Prepare the Sandwich:**
   - Preheat your oven to 375°F (190°C).

- Spread Dijon mustard on one side of each bread slice.
- Spoon the beef bourguignon mixture onto one slice of bread.
- Top with shredded Gruyère or Swiss cheese.
- Place the other bread slice on top to form a sandwich.

3. **Bake the Sandwich:**
   - Place the assembled sandwiches on a baking sheet.
   - Bake for 10-15 minutes, or until the cheese is melted and bubbly and the bread is golden brown.
4. **Serve:**
   - Garnish with fresh parsley if desired.
   - Cut the sandwich into sections and serve hot.

This Beef Bourguignon Sandwich captures the rich flavors of the classic French stew in a delicious, melty sandwich. Enjoy!

Roasted Vegetable Panini

Ingredients:

- 1 loaf ciabatta or focaccia bread
- 2 tbsp olive oil
- 1 red bell pepper, sliced
- 1 yellow bell pepper, sliced
- 1 zucchini, sliced
- 1 eggplant, sliced
- 1 red onion, sliced
- 2 cloves garlic, minced
- Salt and black pepper to taste
- 4 oz (115g) goat cheese or provolone cheese
- 1/4 cup pesto sauce (store-bought or homemade)
- Fresh basil leaves (optional)

Instructions:

1. **Roast the Vegetables:**
   - Preheat your oven to 400°F (200°C).
   - Toss the red bell pepper, yellow bell pepper, zucchini, eggplant, and red onion with olive oil, minced garlic, salt, and black pepper.
   - Spread the vegetables on a baking sheet in a single layer.
   - Roast for 20-25 minutes, or until the vegetables are tender and slightly caramelized, stirring halfway through.
2. **Prepare the Panini:**
   - Slice the ciabatta or focaccia loaf in half horizontally.
   - Spread pesto sauce evenly on the cut sides of the bread.
   - Layer the roasted vegetables over one half of the bread.
   - Top with slices of goat cheese or provolone cheese.
3. **Grill the Panini:**
   - Close the sandwich with the other half of the bread.
   - Preheat a panini press or skillet over medium heat.
   - If using a skillet, place the sandwich in the pan and press down with a heavy pan or a panini press. Cook for about 3-4 minutes per side, or until the bread is golden and the cheese is melted.
   - If using a panini press, cook according to the manufacturer's instructions until the sandwich is crispy and the cheese is melted.
4. **Serve:**
   - Slice the panini into sections.
   - Garnish with fresh basil leaves if desired.

This Roasted Vegetable Panini is flavorful and satisfying, combining sweet roasted vegetables with tangy cheese and aromatic pesto. Enjoy!

Chicken Provençal Sandwich

Ingredients:

For the Chicken:

- 2 boneless, skinless chicken breasts
- 2 tbsp olive oil
- 1 tbsp Herbes de Provence
- 2 cloves garlic, minced
- 1 tbsp lemon juice
- Salt and black pepper to taste

For the Sandwich:

- 4 slices of ciabatta or baguette
- 1/4 cup black olives (Kalamata or Niçoise), pitted and sliced
- 1/4 cup sun-dried tomatoes, sliced
- 1/4 cup roasted red peppers, sliced
- 1/4 cup crumbled feta cheese or goat cheese
- Fresh basil or arugula for garnish
- 2 tbsp Dijon mustard or mayonnaise (optional)

Instructions:

1. **Prepare the Chicken:**
    - Preheat your grill or stovetop grill pan over medium-high heat.
    - In a bowl, mix olive oil, Herbes de Provence, minced garlic, lemon juice, salt, and black pepper.
    - Coat the chicken breasts with the mixture.
    - Grill the chicken for about 6-7 minutes per side, or until fully cooked and the internal temperature reaches 165°F (74°C). Let the chicken rest for a few minutes, then slice it thinly.
2. **Prepare the Bread:**
    - Toast the ciabatta or baguette slices if desired.
3. **Assemble the Sandwich:**
    - If using, spread Dijon mustard or mayonnaise on one side of each slice of bread.
    - Layer the sliced chicken on one slice of bread.
    - Top with black olives, sun-dried tomatoes, roasted red peppers, and crumbled feta or goat cheese.
    - Add fresh basil or arugula for a burst of freshness.
4. **Serve:**
    - Close the sandwich with the remaining slice of bread.
    - Cut into sections if desired and serve immediately.

This Chicken Provençal Sandwich combines the rich, aromatic flavors of Provençal cuisine with tender grilled chicken and Mediterranean ingredients. Enjoy!

French Dip Sandwich

Ingredients:

For the Beef:

- 1 lb (450g) beef chuck roast or sirloin
- 2 tbsp olive oil
- 1 onion, sliced
- 2 cloves garlic, minced
- 1 cup beef broth
- 1 cup water
- 1/2 cup dry white wine (optional)
- 1 tbsp Worcestershire sauce
- 1 tbsp soy sauce
- 1 bay leaf
- 1 tsp dried thyme
- Salt and black pepper to taste

For the Sandwich:

- 4 hoagie rolls or French baguettes
- 4 slices provolone or Swiss cheese (optional)
- 2 tbsp Dijon mustard (optional)

Instructions:

1. **Prepare the Beef:**
    - Season the beef with salt and black pepper.
    - Heat olive oil in a large skillet or Dutch oven over medium-high heat.
    - Sear the beef on all sides until browned. Remove from the pan and set aside.
2. **Make the Broth:**
    - In the same pan, add sliced onion and cook until softened.
    - Add minced garlic and cook for another minute.
    - Pour in the beef broth, water, and white wine (if using). Stir in Worcestershire sauce, soy sauce, bay leaf, and thyme.
    - Return the beef to the pan, making sure it's partially submerged in the liquid.
    - Bring to a boil, then reduce heat to low and simmer, covered, for about 2-3 hours, or until the beef is tender and easily shreds with a fork.
3. **Prepare the Sandwich:**
    - Preheat your oven to 375°F (190°C).
    - Remove the beef from the broth and shred it with two forks. Discard any large pieces of fat.
    - Place the shredded beef back in the broth to keep warm.

- Slice the hoagie rolls or baguettes and optionally spread with Dijon mustard.
   - If using cheese, place a slice of cheese on the bottom half of each roll.
4. **Assemble and Toast the Sandwiches:**
   - Using a slotted spoon, load the shredded beef onto the rolls.
   - Bake in the preheated oven for about 5-7 minutes, or until the cheese is melted and the bread is toasted.
5. **Serve:**
   - Serve the sandwiches with a small bowl of the beef broth for dipping (au jus).

This French Dip Sandwich is a delicious, hearty meal with tender beef and flavorful broth. Enjoy!

Smoked Salmon and Cream Cheese Baguette

Ingredients:

- 1 French baguette
- 4 oz (115g) cream cheese, softened
- 4 oz (115g) smoked salmon
- 1/2 small red onion, thinly sliced
- 1/4 cup capers, drained
- 1/2 cucumber, thinly sliced
- Fresh dill or chives for garnish
- Lemon wedges for serving (optional)
- Freshly ground black pepper to taste

Instructions:

1. **Prepare the Baguette:**
    - Slice the baguette lengthwise but not all the way through—leave a hinge.
    - If desired, lightly toast the inside of the baguette slices under a broiler or in a toaster oven until golden.
2. **Prepare the Spread:**
    - Spread a generous layer of softened cream cheese evenly on both sides of the baguette.
3. **Assemble the Sandwich:**
    - Layer the smoked salmon over the cream cheese.
    - Arrange the thinly sliced red onion on top of the salmon.
    - Scatter capers over the onions.
    - Place cucumber slices on top of the capers.
    - Garnish with fresh dill or chives and season with freshly ground black pepper.
4. **Serve:**
    - Close the baguette, cut into sections if desired, and serve immediately.
    - Optionally, serve with lemon wedges on the side for a touch of extra flavor.

This Smoked Salmon and Cream Cheese Baguette is a delicious and elegant option for brunch or a light lunch, combining creamy, savory, and fresh flavors. Enjoy!

Alsatian Tartine

Ingredients:

- 4 slices of crusty bread (such as country bread or baguette)
- 1 cup (200g) Gruyère cheese, shredded (or a combination of Gruyère and Emmental)
- 1/2 cup (120g) crème fraîche or sour cream
- 1/4 cup (60ml) heavy cream
- 1 medium onion, thinly sliced
- 2 tbsp unsalted butter
- 4 oz (115g) ham, thinly sliced (or bacon lardons)
- 1 tbsp Dijon mustard (optional)
- Freshly ground black pepper to taste
- Fresh thyme or parsley for garnish (optional)

Instructions:

1. **Prepare the Onions:**
    - Heat butter in a skillet over medium heat.
    - Add the sliced onions and cook, stirring frequently, until they are caramelized and golden brown (about 15-20 minutes). Set aside.
2. **Prepare the Cream Mixture:**
    - In a bowl, combine the crème fraîche or sour cream with the heavy cream.
    - Mix in the shredded Gruyère cheese. Season with freshly ground black pepper.
3. **Assemble the Tartines:**
    - Preheat your oven to 375°F (190°C).
    - If desired, spread a thin layer of Dijon mustard on each slice of bread.
    - Spread the cheese mixture evenly over the bread slices.
    - Top with the caramelized onions and sliced ham (or bacon lardons).
4. **Bake the Tartines:**
    - Place the assembled tartines on a baking sheet.
    - Bake in the preheated oven for 10-15 minutes, or until the cheese is melted and bubbly, and the bread is crisp.
5. **Serve:**
    - Garnish with fresh thyme or parsley if desired.
    - Cut into portions and serve hot.

This Alsatian Tartine is a savory and comforting dish, perfect for a hearty snack or light meal. Enjoy!

Pork and Apple Chutney Sandwich

Ingredients:

For the Sandwich:

- 2 cups cooked pork (e.g., pork roast or tenderloin), sliced or shredded
- 1/2 cup apple chutney (store-bought or homemade)
- 4 slices of crusty bread (such as ciabatta or sourdough)
- 1/4 cup Dijon mustard (optional)
- 4 oz (115g) sharp cheddar cheese, sliced (optional)
- Fresh arugula or spinach for garnish (optional)

For Homemade Apple Chutney (optional):

- 2 apples, peeled, cored, and diced
- 1/2 cup onions, diced
- 1/2 cup raisins
- 1/4 cup apple cider vinegar
- 1/4 cup brown sugar
- 1 tsp ground ginger
- 1/2 tsp ground cinnamon
- Salt to taste

Instructions:

For Homemade Apple Chutney:

1. **Cook the Chutney:**
   - In a saucepan, combine apples, onions, raisins, apple cider vinegar, brown sugar, ginger, cinnamon, and a pinch of salt.
   - Bring to a boil, then reduce heat and simmer for 20-25 minutes, stirring occasionally, until the chutney thickens and the apples are tender. Let cool before using.

For the Sandwich:

1. **Prepare the Bread:**
   - Toast the bread slices lightly if desired.
2. **Assemble the Sandwich:**
   - Spread Dijon mustard on one side of each slice of bread, if using.
   - Layer the cooked pork on one slice of bread.
   - Top with apple chutney.
   - Add sliced cheddar cheese if desired.

3. **Grill or Serve:**
    - For a warm sandwich, place the assembled sandwich in a hot skillet or panini press and cook until the cheese is melted and the bread is golden brown.
    - Alternatively, serve the sandwich as is, with fresh arugula or spinach for added crunch.
4. **Serve:**
    - Cut the sandwich in half if desired and serve immediately.

This Pork and Apple Chutney Sandwich blends savory pork with the sweet and tangy notes of apple chutney for a delicious and satisfying meal. Enjoy!

Caramelized Onion and Goat Cheese Baguette

Ingredients:

- 1 French baguette
- 2 tbsp olive oil
- 2 large onions, thinly sliced
- 4 oz (115g) goat cheese, softened
- 2 tbsp honey (optional, for extra sweetness)
- Fresh thyme or parsley for garnish (optional)
- Salt and black pepper to taste

Instructions:

1. **Caramelize the Onions:**
    - Heat olive oil in a skillet over medium heat.
    - Add the sliced onions and cook, stirring frequently, until they are deeply caramelized and golden brown (about 20-25 minutes). Season with salt and black pepper to taste.
    - Stir in honey if using, and cook for an additional minute.
2. **Prepare the Baguette:**
    - Preheat your oven to 375°F (190°C).
    - Slice the baguette in half lengthwise.
    - If desired, lightly toast the cut sides under the broiler or in a toaster oven until golden.
3. **Assemble the Baguette:**
    - Spread the softened goat cheese evenly over the cut sides of the baguette.
    - Top with the caramelized onions, spreading them evenly.
4. **Bake the Baguette:**
    - Place the assembled baguette on a baking sheet.
    - Bake in the preheated oven for 5-10 minutes, or until the cheese is slightly melted and the bread is crispy.
5. **Garnish and Serve:**
    - Garnish with fresh thyme or parsley if desired.
    - Cut into sections and serve warm.

This Caramelized Onion and Goat Cheese Baguette is a flavorful and elegant option for a snack or appetizer. Enjoy!

Steak Frites Sandwich

Ingredients:

For the Steak:

- 1 lb (450g) sirloin steak or flank steak
- 2 tbsp olive oil
- 2 cloves garlic, minced
- 1 tbsp fresh rosemary or thyme, chopped (or 1 tsp dried)
- Salt and black pepper to taste

For the Fries:

- 2 large russet potatoes, peeled and cut into thin strips
- 2 tbsp olive oil
- Salt to taste

For the Sandwich:

- 4 slices of crusty bread (such as ciabatta or baguette)
- 2 tbsp Dijon mustard or mayonnaise (optional)
- 1/4 cup ketchup (optional)
- Fresh arugula or lettuce for garnish (optional)

Instructions:

1. **Prepare the Fries:**
   - Preheat your oven to 425°F (220°C).
   - Toss the potato strips with olive oil and salt.
   - Spread them out in a single layer on a baking sheet.
   - Bake for 25-30 minutes, turning halfway through, until crispy and golden brown.
2. **Prepare the Steak:**
   - Preheat a grill or skillet over medium-high heat.
   - Rub the steak with olive oil, minced garlic, rosemary or thyme, salt, and black pepper.
   - Grill or cook the steak for about 4-5 minutes per side for medium-rare, or to your desired doneness.
   - Let the steak rest for 5 minutes before slicing thinly against the grain.
3. **Prepare the Bread:**
   - Toast the bread slices lightly if desired.
4. **Assemble the Sandwich:**
   - If using, spread Dijon mustard or mayonnaise on one side of each slice of bread.
   - Layer the sliced steak evenly on the bread.

        - Top with the baked fries. You can add ketchup if desired.
        - Add fresh arugula or lettuce for a bit of freshness if using.
5. **Serve:**
        - Close the sandwich with the other slice of bread.
        - Cut into sections if desired and serve immediately.

This Steak Frites Sandwich offers the satisfying combination of tender steak and crispy fries, all in a hearty sandwich. Enjoy!

Quiche Lorraine Sandwich

Ingredients:

For the Quiche Lorraine:

- 1 pre-made pie crust or homemade pie dough
- 6 oz (170g) bacon or pancetta, diced
- 1/2 cup (120ml) heavy cream
- 1/2 cup (120ml) milk
- 3 large eggs
- 1 cup (115g) Gruyère or Swiss cheese, shredded
- 1/2 cup (50g) Parmesan cheese, grated
- 1/2 cup (60g) onion, finely chopped
- Salt and black pepper to taste
- Freshly grated nutmeg (optional)

For the Sandwich:

- 4 slices of crusty bread (such as ciabatta or sourdough)
- 2 tbsp Dijon mustard or mayonnaise (optional)
- Fresh arugula or spinach (optional)

Instructions:

1. **Prepare the Quiche Lorraine:**
    - **Preheat the Oven:** Preheat your oven to 375°F (190°C).
    - **Cook the Bacon:** In a skillet, cook the diced bacon or pancetta over medium heat until crispy. Remove and drain on paper towels. Discard excess fat.
    - **Prepare the Pie Crust:** Place the pie crust in a tart pan or pie dish, pressing it into the edges. Prick the bottom with a fork.
    - **Prepare the Filling:** In a bowl, whisk together heavy cream, milk, and eggs. Stir in the Gruyère or Swiss cheese, Parmesan cheese, and cooked bacon. Season with salt, black pepper, and a pinch of freshly grated nutmeg if using.
    - **Cook the Onion:** In the same skillet used for bacon, cook the chopped onion until softened and translucent. Add to the quiche filling mixture.
    - **Bake the Quiche:** Pour the filling into the pie crust and bake for 30-35 minutes, or until the quiche is set and lightly browned on top. Allow it to cool slightly before slicing.
2. **Prepare the Sandwich:**
    - **Toast the Bread:** Lightly toast the bread slices if desired.
    - **Spread:** Optionally spread Dijon mustard or mayonnaise on one side of each slice of bread.

- **Assemble:** Layer slices of the cooled quiche Lorraine on one side of the bread. Add fresh arugula or spinach if desired.
3. **Serve:**
    - **Close and Slice:** Top with the remaining slice of bread to make a sandwich. Cut into sections if desired and serve immediately.

This Quiche Lorraine Sandwich brings together the savory flavors of the classic quiche into a portable and satisfying sandwich. Enjoy!

Lobster Roll à la Française

Ingredients:

For the Lobster Filling:

- 1 lb (450g) lobster meat, cooked and chopped (fresh or thawed from frozen)
- 1/4 cup mayonnaise
- 1 tbsp Dijon mustard
- 1 tbsp fresh tarragon, chopped (or 1 tsp dried)
- 1 tbsp fresh lemon juice
- 1 tbsp finely chopped chives or scallions
- Salt and black pepper to taste

For the Rolls:

- 4 split-top hot dog buns or brioche rolls
- 2 tbsp unsalted butter
- Fresh chives or tarragon for garnish (optional)
- Lemon wedges for serving (optional)

Instructions:

1. **Prepare the Lobster Filling:**
    - In a bowl, combine the mayonnaise, Dijon mustard, tarragon, lemon juice, and chives or scallions.
    - Gently fold in the chopped lobster meat.
    - Season with salt and black pepper to taste. Chill in the refrigerator while you prepare the rolls.
2. **Prepare the Rolls:**
    - Heat butter in a skillet over medium heat.
    - Lightly butter the cut sides of each roll.
    - Toast the rolls in the skillet until golden brown and crispy.
3. **Assemble the Lobster Rolls:**
    - Spoon the lobster mixture generously into each toasted roll.
    - Garnish with additional fresh chives or tarragon if desired.
4. **Serve:**
    - Serve the lobster rolls with lemon wedges on the side for a touch of brightness.

This Lobster Roll à la Française features a creamy, herb-infused lobster filling nestled in a buttery, toasted roll, offering a refined twist on the classic seafood sandwich. Enjoy!

Foie Gras and Fig Sandwich

Ingredients:

- 1 baguette or crusty country bread
- 2-4 oz (60-115g) foie gras (or pâté if unavailable)
- 1/4 cup fig jam or preserves
- 2 tbsp unsalted butter
- Fresh arugula or baby spinach (optional)
- Salt and black pepper to taste

Instructions:

1. **Prepare the Bread:**
    - Slice the baguette or bread into sandwich-sized pieces.
    - Lightly toast the slices if desired.
2. **Prepare the Foie Gras:**
    - If using foie gras slices, sear in a hot, dry skillet over medium-high heat for 1-2 minutes per side, or until golden and slightly crispy on the outside.
    - If using foie gras pâté, it can be spread directly without further preparation.
3. **Assemble the Sandwich:**
    - Spread fig jam evenly on one side of each slice of bread.
    - Spread or layer foie gras on top of the fig jam.
    - Season with a touch of salt and black pepper if desired.
    - Add fresh arugula or baby spinach if using.
4. **Serve:**
    - Close the sandwich with the remaining bread slice.
    - Cut into sections if desired and serve immediately.

This Foie Gras and Fig Sandwich combines the rich, luxurious flavor of foie gras with the sweet contrast of fig jam, creating a gourmet experience. Enjoy!

Grilled Cheese with Tomato and Basil

Ingredients:

- 4 slices of your favorite bread (such as sourdough, ciabatta, or whole grain)
- 4 oz (115g) sharp cheddar cheese, sliced or shredded
- 4 oz (115g) mozzarella cheese, sliced or shredded
- 1-2 ripe tomatoes, sliced
- 1/4 cup fresh basil leaves
- 2 tbsp unsalted butter
- 1-2 cloves garlic, minced (optional, for extra flavor)
- Salt and black pepper to taste

Instructions:

1. **Prepare the Ingredients:**
   - Slice the bread if it isn't pre-sliced.
   - Slice the tomatoes and pat them dry with paper towels to remove excess moisture.
   - If using, mix minced garlic with the softened butter.
2. **Assemble the Sandwich:**
   - Butter one side of each slice of bread. If using garlic butter, spread a thin layer of garlic butter on one side of each slice.
   - On the unbuttered side of two slices, layer the cheddar and mozzarella cheese.
   - Add tomato slices on top of the cheese.
   - Scatter fresh basil leaves over the tomatoes.
   - Season with salt and black pepper to taste.
   - Top with the remaining slices of bread, buttered side up.
3. **Grill the Sandwich:**
   - Heat a skillet or griddle over medium heat.
   - Place the sandwiches in the skillet and cook for 3-4 minutes on each side, or until the bread is golden brown and the cheese is melted. Press down lightly with a spatula for even grilling.
4. **Serve:**
   - Remove from heat and let cool for a minute before slicing.
   - Cut into halves or quarters if desired and serve immediately.

This Grilled Cheese with Tomato and Basil is a classic and comforting sandwich with a fresh twist. Enjoy the blend of melty cheeses, juicy tomatoes, and fragrant basil!

Salami and Emmental Baguette

Ingredients:

- 1 French baguette
- 4 oz (115g) Emmental cheese, sliced
- 4 oz (115g) salami, thinly sliced
- 2 tbsp Dijon mustard or mayonnaise (optional)
- 1/2 cup mixed greens or arugula (optional)
- 1-2 tomatoes, thinly sliced (optional)
- 1/4 cup pickles or cornichons, sliced (optional)
- Freshly ground black pepper to taste

Instructions:

1. **Prepare the Baguette:**
    - Slice the baguette in half lengthwise.
    - If desired, lightly toast the cut sides under the broiler or in a toaster oven until golden.
2. **Prepare the Spread:**
    - Spread Dijon mustard or mayonnaise on one side of each slice of the baguette if using.
3. **Assemble the Sandwich:**
    - Layer the Emmental cheese evenly on the bottom half of the baguette.
    - Top with slices of salami.
    - Add mixed greens or arugula if using.
    - Layer with tomato slices and pickles or cornichons if desired.
    - Season with freshly ground black pepper to taste.
4. **Serve:**
    - Close the sandwich with the top half of the baguette.
    - Cut into sections if desired and serve immediately.

This Salami and Emmental Baguette combines the rich, nutty flavor of Emmental cheese with savory salami for a satisfying and classic sandwich. Enjoy!

Chicken and Tarragon Sandwich

Ingredients:

- 2 cups cooked chicken, shredded or diced (such as roasted or poached)
- 1/4 cup mayonnaise
- 1 tbsp fresh tarragon, chopped (or 1 tsp dried)
- 1 tbsp Dijon mustard
- 1 celery stalk, finely chopped
- 1/4 cup red onion, finely chopped (optional)
- Salt and black pepper to taste
- 4 slices of bread (such as whole grain, ciabatta, or sourdough)
- Lettuce or arugula for garnish (optional)

Instructions:

1. **Prepare the Chicken Mixture:**
    - In a bowl, combine the mayonnaise, chopped tarragon, Dijon mustard, and season with salt and black pepper.
    - Fold in the shredded or diced chicken, chopped celery, and red onion if using.
2. **Assemble the Sandwich:**
    - Spread the chicken mixture evenly over two slices of bread.
    - Add lettuce or arugula if desired.
    - Top with the remaining bread slices.
3. **Serve:**
    - Cut the sandwiches in half if desired and serve immediately.

This Chicken and Tarragon Sandwich is fresh and flavorful, with a hint of herbal elegance from the tarragon. Enjoy!

Ratatouille and Mozzarella Panini

Ingredients:

- 1 loaf of ciabatta or another crusty bread
- 1 cup ratatouille (store-bought or homemade)
- 4 oz (115g) mozzarella cheese, sliced or shredded
- 2 tbsp olive oil
- 1 clove garlic, minced (optional)
- Fresh basil leaves (optional)
- Salt and black pepper to taste

Instructions:

1. **Prepare the Ratatouille:**
   - If using homemade ratatouille, make sure it's well-seasoned and heated. If store-bought, warm it up as per package instructions.
2. **Prepare the Panini:**
   - Slice the ciabatta loaf in half lengthwise.
   - If using, mix minced garlic with olive oil and brush the cut sides of the bread with it.
   - On the bottom half of the bread, spread the warmed ratatouille evenly.
   - Layer with mozzarella cheese.
   - Top with fresh basil leaves if desired, and season with salt and black pepper.
3. **Grill the Panini:**
   - Close the sandwich with the top half of the bread.
   - Heat a panini press or skillet over medium heat.
   - Brush the outside of the bread with olive oil.
   - Grill the sandwich in the panini press or skillet, pressing down gently, until the bread is crispy and golden, and the cheese is melted (about 4-6 minutes).
4. **Serve:**
   - Cut the panini in half if desired and serve warm.

This Ratatouille and Mozzarella Panini combines the rich, savory flavors of ratatouille with the creamy melt of mozzarella for a deliciously satisfying sandwich. Enjoy!

Roasted Chicken and Avocado Baguette

Ingredients:

- 1 French baguette
- 1 cup roasted chicken, shredded or sliced
- 1 ripe avocado, sliced
- 2 tbsp mayonnaise or Greek yogurt
- 1 tbsp lemon juice
- 1 cup mixed greens or arugula
- 1 small tomato, sliced (optional)
- Salt and black pepper to taste

Instructions:

1. **Prepare the Avocado Spread:**
   - In a bowl, mash the avocado with lemon juice, salt, and black pepper.
2. **Prepare the Baguette:**
   - Slice the baguette in half lengthwise.
   - Lightly toast the cut sides if desired.
3. **Assemble the Sandwich:**
   - Spread mayonnaise or Greek yogurt on the cut sides of the baguette.
   - Layer the roasted chicken evenly on the bottom half of the baguette.
   - Top with avocado slices.
   - Add mixed greens or arugula and tomato slices if using.
4. **Serve:**
   - Close the baguette with the top half.
   - Cut into sections if desired and serve immediately.

This Roasted Chicken and Avocado Baguette is a fresh and satisfying sandwich with creamy avocado and juicy chicken. Enjoy!

Ham, Egg, and Cheese Croissant

Ingredients:

- 2 large croissants
- 4 slices of ham
- 2 large eggs
- 2 oz (60g) cheddar or Swiss cheese, sliced
- 1 tbsp butter
- Salt and black pepper to taste
- Fresh chives or parsley for garnish (optional)

Instructions:

1. **Prepare the Croissants:**
    - Preheat your oven to 350°F (175°C).
    - Slice the croissants in half horizontally, but do not cut all the way through.
2. **Cook the Eggs:**
    - Heat butter in a nonstick skillet over medium heat.
    - Crack the eggs into the skillet and cook to your desired doneness (sunny-side up, scrambled, etc.), seasoning with salt and black pepper.
3. **Assemble the Croissants:**
    - Place a slice of cheese on the bottom half of each croissant.
    - Layer with slices of ham.
    - Top with cooked eggs.
4. **Bake the Croissants:**
    - Close the croissants and place them on a baking sheet.
    - Bake in the preheated oven for 5-7 minutes, or until the cheese is melted and the croissant is warmed through.
5. **Serve:**
    - Garnish with fresh chives or parsley if desired.
    - Serve immediately while warm.

This Ham, Egg, and Cheese Croissant is a delightful and indulgent breakfast or brunch option. Enjoy!

French Country Pâté Sandwich

Ingredients:

- 1 baguette or rustic country bread
- 4 oz (115g) French country pâté (such as pâté de campagne)
- 2-3 tbsp Dijon mustard
- 4-6 cornichons or pickles, sliced
- 1/4 cup thinly sliced red onion
- Fresh parsley or arugula for garnish (optional)
- Salt and black pepper to taste

Instructions:

1. **Prepare the Bread:**
   - Slice the baguette or country bread in half lengthwise.
2. **Assemble the Sandwich:**
   - Spread Dijon mustard evenly on one side of each slice of bread.
   - Layer the pâté evenly over the mustard on one slice of bread.
   - Top with sliced cornichons and red onion.
   - Season with salt and black pepper if desired.
   - Add fresh parsley or arugula for a touch of freshness, if using.
3. **Serve:**
   - Close the sandwich with the other slice of bread.
   - Cut into sections if desired and serve immediately.

This French Country Pâté Sandwich combines the rich flavors of pâté with the tangy bite of mustard and pickles for a classic and satisfying meal. Enjoy!

Black Truffle and Mushroom Baguette

Ingredients:

- 1 French baguette
- 8 oz (225g) mixed mushrooms (such as cremini, shiitake, or button), sliced
- 2 tbsp olive oil
- 2 cloves garlic, minced
- 1-2 tbsp black truffle oil (to taste)
- 1 tbsp fresh thyme or rosemary, chopped (or 1 tsp dried)
- 2 oz (60g) Gruyère or Parmesan cheese, grated (optional)
- Salt and black pepper to taste
- Fresh parsley for garnish (optional)

Instructions:

1. **Prepare the Mushrooms:**
    - Heat olive oil in a skillet over medium-high heat.
    - Add the sliced mushrooms and cook, stirring occasionally, until they are golden brown and tender (about 5-7 minutes).
    - Add minced garlic and cook for an additional minute.
    - Stir in the black truffle oil and fresh thyme or rosemary.
    - Season with salt and black pepper to taste.
    - Remove from heat and set aside.
2. **Prepare the Baguette:**
    - Preheat your oven to 375°F (190°C).
    - Slice the baguette in half lengthwise.
    - Optionally, lightly toast the cut sides under the broiler or in a toaster oven until golden.
3. **Assemble the Baguette:**
    - Spoon the cooked mushroom mixture evenly over the bottom half of the baguette.
    - Sprinkle with grated Gruyère or Parmesan cheese if desired.
    - Place the assembled baguette on a baking sheet.
4. **Bake:**
    - Bake in the preheated oven for 5-10 minutes, or until the cheese is melted and bubbly and the bread is crispy.
5. **Serve:**
    - Garnish with fresh parsley if desired.
    - Cut into sections and serve warm.

This Black Truffle and Mushroom Baguette is a luxurious and flavorful treat, perfect for an elegant appetizer or a satisfying snack. Enjoy!

Baked Brie and Apple Sandwich

Ingredients:

- 1 baguette or ciabatta loaf
- 4 oz (115g) Brie cheese, sliced
- 1 apple (such as Honeycrisp or Fuji), thinly sliced
- 2 tbsp honey or fig jam
- 1-2 tbsp unsalted butter
- Fresh arugula or spinach (optional)
- Fresh thyme or rosemary (optional)
- Salt and black pepper to taste

Instructions:

1. **Prepare the Bread:**
    - Preheat your oven to 375°F (190°C).
    - Slice the baguette or ciabatta loaf in half lengthwise.
2. **Assemble the Sandwich:**
    - Spread honey or fig jam evenly on one side of each slice of bread.
    - Layer the Brie cheese slices on one half of the bread.
    - Arrange the apple slices on top of the Brie.
    - Add fresh arugula or spinach if using.
    - Season with a bit of salt and black pepper.
    - Sprinkle with fresh thyme or rosemary if desired.
3. **Bake the Sandwich:**
    - Close the sandwich with the other half of the bread.
    - Butter the outside of the bread slices lightly.
    - Place the sandwich on a baking sheet.
4. **Bake:**
    - Bake in the preheated oven for 10-12 minutes, or until the bread is golden and crispy and the Brie is melted.
5. **Serve:**
    - Cut into sections if desired and serve warm.

This Baked Brie and Apple Sandwich combines creamy Brie with sweet apples and honey for a deliciously satisfying treat. Enjoy!

Provençal Tuna Sandwich

Ingredients:

For the Sandwich:

- 1 can (5-6 oz) of high-quality tuna in olive oil, drained
- 1 tablespoon capers, rinsed and chopped
- 1 tablespoon black olives, pitted and chopped
- 1 small shallot, finely chopped
- 1 tablespoon fresh parsley, chopped
- 1 tablespoon fresh basil, chopped (or a pinch of dried basil)
- 1 tablespoon lemon juice
- 2 tablespoons extra-virgin olive oil
- Salt and freshly ground black pepper, to taste
- 1-2 tablespoons Dijon mustard (optional, for extra flavor)
- 4 slices of rustic bread (like ciabatta or sourdough), lightly toasted
- 1 ripe tomato, sliced
- 1 small cucumber, sliced
- 1 small handful of arugula or mixed greens

For the Provençal Touch:

- 1 clove garlic, minced (optional, for rubbing on bread)
- A few thin slices of red onion (optional, for extra crunch)

Instructions:

1. **Prepare the Tuna Mixture:**
   - In a bowl, combine the drained tuna, capers, olives, shallot, parsley, and basil.
   - Stir in the lemon juice and olive oil.
   - Season with salt and pepper to taste. If using Dijon mustard, mix it in for extra tanginess.
2. **Toast the Bread:**
   - Lightly toast the slices of bread. If you like, you can rub a cut garlic clove on the warm bread for added flavor.
3. **Assemble the Sandwich:**
   - Spread the tuna mixture evenly on two slices of bread.
   - Top with tomato slices, cucumber slices, and a handful of arugula or mixed greens.
   - Add thin slices of red onion if using.
   - Place the remaining slices of bread on top.
4. **Serve:**
   - Cut the sandwiches in half and serve immediately.

This Provençal Tuna Sandwich is not only tasty but also easy to put together. It's perfect for a quick lunch or a light dinner, bringing a bit of Southern French flair to your table. Enjoy!

Roasted Tomato and Basil Panini

Ingredients:

- 4 ripe tomatoes, halved
- 2 tablespoons olive oil
- Salt and pepper, to taste
- 2 cloves garlic, minced
- 1 teaspoon dried oregano or a few fresh oregano leaves
- 4 slices of ciabatta or sourdough bread
- 2 tablespoons pesto (store-bought or homemade)
- 1 cup fresh basil leaves
- 4 oz fresh mozzarella or provolone cheese, sliced
- Balsamic glaze (optional, for drizzling)

Instructions:

1. **Roast the Tomatoes:**
   - Preheat the oven to 375°F (190°C).
   - Place the tomato halves on a baking sheet, drizzle with olive oil, and sprinkle with salt, pepper, garlic, and oregano.
   - Roast for about 25-30 minutes, until tomatoes are soft and caramelized.
2. **Assemble the Panini:**
   - Spread pesto on one side of each bread slice.
   - Layer roasted tomatoes, fresh basil leaves, and cheese on two of the bread slices.
   - Top with the remaining bread slices, pesto side down.
3. **Grill the Panini:**
   - Heat a panini press or grill pan over medium heat.
   - Grill the sandwiches for 3-4 minutes per side, or until the bread is crispy and the cheese is melted.
4. **Serve:**
   - Drizzle with balsamic glaze if desired.
   - Cut and serve warm.

This panini captures the ultimate essence of summer with the roasted tomatoes and fresh basil, perfect for a satisfying meal. Enjoy!

Smoked Duck and Cranberry Sandwich

Ingredients:

- 8 oz smoked duck breast, sliced
- 1/2 cup cranberry sauce (store-bought or homemade)
- 4 slices of rustic bread (like rye or sourdough)
- 1 cup arugula or spinach
- 1 small red onion, thinly sliced
- 2 tablespoons Dijon mustard
- 1 tablespoon olive oil
- Salt and pepper, to taste

Instructions:

1. **Prepare the Bread:**
   - Lightly toast the bread slices if desired.
2. **Assemble the Sandwich:**
   - Spread Dijon mustard on one side of each bread slice.
   - Spread cranberry sauce on two of the bread slices.
   - Layer smoked duck slices on top of the cranberry sauce.
   - Add arugula and red onion slices.
   - Season with a little salt and pepper.
3. **Finish the Sandwich:**
   - Top with the remaining bread slices, mustard side down.
   - Optionally, you can brush the outside of the bread with olive oil and grill the sandwich for a crispier texture.
4. **Serve:**
   - Cut the sandwich in half and serve immediately.

This sandwich combines the ultimate savory and sweet elements, making for a delightful and gourmet treat. Enjoy!

Savory Herb and Goat Cheese Tartine

Ingredients:

- 4 slices of crusty bread (like sourdough or ciabatta)
- 4 oz goat cheese, softened
- 2 tablespoons olive oil
- 1 tablespoon fresh thyme leaves (or 1 teaspoon dried thyme)
- 1 tablespoon fresh rosemary, chopped (or 1 teaspoon dried rosemary)
- 1 garlic clove, minced
- Salt and pepper, to taste
- Optional: thinly sliced radishes or cherry tomatoes for garnish

Instructions:

1. **Prepare the Bread:**
    - Preheat the oven to 375°F (190°C).
    - Brush both sides of the bread slices with olive oil.
    - Arrange on a baking sheet and toast in the oven for about 5-7 minutes, until golden and crispy.
2. **Prepare the Goat Cheese Spread:**
    - In a bowl, mix the softened goat cheese with thyme, rosemary, minced garlic, salt, and pepper.
3. **Assemble the Tartine:**
    - Spread the herb and goat cheese mixture evenly over the toasted bread slices.
4. **Finish and Serve:**
    - Optionally, top with thinly sliced radishes or cherry tomatoes for extra freshness and crunch.
    - Serve immediately while the bread is still crispy.

This tartine offers a delightful blend of creamy goat cheese and aromatic herbs on a crispy base, making it perfect for a light lunch or appetizer. Enjoy!

Shrimp and Avocado Baguette

Ingredients:

- 1 baguette, sliced lengthwise
- 1 pound cooked shrimp, peeled and deveined
- 1 avocado, sliced
- 1 tablespoon olive oil
- 1 tablespoon lemon juice
- 1 teaspoon smoked paprika
- 1 clove garlic, minced
- 1 cup mixed greens or arugula
- Salt and pepper, to taste
- Optional: a few sprigs of fresh cilantro or parsley for garnish

Instructions:

1. **Prepare the Shrimp:**
    - In a bowl, toss the cooked shrimp with olive oil, lemon juice, smoked paprika, minced garlic, salt, and pepper.
2. **Assemble the Baguette:**
    - Lightly toast the baguette slices if desired.
    - Arrange the avocado slices evenly on the baguette.
3. **Top with Shrimp:**
    - Place the seasoned shrimp on top of the avocado.
4. **Add Greens:**
    - Top with mixed greens or arugula.
5. **Finish and Serve:**
    - Garnish with fresh cilantro or parsley if using.
    - Serve immediately.

This baguette combines the ultimate freshness of shrimp and avocado, creating a deliciously light yet satisfying meal. Enjoy!

Beef and Blue Cheese Sandwich

Ingredients:

- 8 oz cooked beef (e.g., steak, roast beef), sliced thinly
- 2 tablespoons blue cheese crumbles
- 4 slices of crusty bread (like ciabatta or sourdough)
- 1 tablespoon butter
- 1 tablespoon mayonnaise
- 1 tablespoon Dijon mustard
- 1 small onion, caramelized
- Arugula or spinach (optional)
- Salt and pepper, to taste

Instructions:

1. **Prepare the Bread:**
    - Spread butter on one side of each bread slice.
    - Heat a skillet over medium heat and toast the bread slices butter-side down until golden brown.
2. **Assemble the Sandwich:**
    - Mix mayonnaise and Dijon mustard, then spread on the unbuttered side of two bread slices.
    - Layer the sliced beef on top of the mayo-mustard spread.
    - Sprinkle blue cheese crumbles over the beef.
    - Add caramelized onions and arugula or spinach if using.
3. **Finish and Serve:**
    - Top with the remaining bread slices.
    - Optionally, grill the sandwich until the cheese is slightly melted.

This sandwich offers the ultimate combination of savory beef and tangy blue cheese, creating a satisfying and flavorful meal. Enjoy!

Duck and Orange Marmalade Panini

Ingredients:

- 8 oz cooked duck breast, thinly sliced (smoked or roasted)
- 1/4 cup orange marmalade
- 4 slices of ciabatta or sourdough bread
- 2 tablespoons Dijon mustard
- 2 oz goat cheese or brie, sliced
- 1 cup baby spinach or arugula
- 1 small red onion, thinly sliced
- 2 tablespoons olive oil

Instructions:

1. **Prepare the Bread:**
   - Preheat your panini press or grill pan.
   - Spread Dijon mustard on one side of each bread slice.
2. **Assemble the Panini:**
   - Spread orange marmalade on top of the Dijon mustard on two of the bread slices.
   - Layer the sliced duck breast over the marmalade.
   - Top with goat cheese or brie, red onion slices, and spinach or arugula.
   - Place the remaining bread slices on top, mustard side down.
3. **Grill the Panini:**
   - Brush the outside of the bread with olive oil.
   - Grill in the panini press or grill pan for 3-4 minutes per side, or until the bread is crispy and the cheese is melted.
4. **Serve:**
   - Cut the panini in half and serve warm.

This panini brings together the rich flavors of duck with the sweet and tangy orange marmalade, offering a gourmet twist on a classic sandwich. Enjoy!

Spinach and Feta Croissant

Ingredients:

- 1 sheet of puff pastry or 2 pre-made croissants
- 1 cup fresh spinach, chopped
- 1/2 cup crumbled feta cheese
- 1/4 cup grated Parmesan cheese
- 1 egg, beaten (for egg wash)
- Salt and pepper, to taste
- 1 tablespoon olive oil (optional, for sautéing)

Instructions:

1. **Prepare the Filling:**
    - If using fresh spinach, sauté it in olive oil until wilted and moisture is reduced. Let cool slightly.
    - In a bowl, mix the spinach with feta cheese, Parmesan, salt, and pepper.
2. **Assemble the Croissant:**
    - If using puff pastry, cut it into squares or rectangles. Place a spoonful of the filling in the center of each square.
    - Fold the pastry over the filling to form a triangle or rectangle, sealing the edges well.
    - If using pre-made croissants, carefully cut them open and fill with the spinach and feta mixture. Close them gently.
3. **Apply Egg Wash:**
    - Brush the top of each croissant or pastry with beaten egg for a golden finish.
4. **Bake:**
    - Preheat the oven to 375°F (190°C).
    - Place the croissants or pastries on a baking sheet lined with parchment paper.
    - Bake for 15-20 minutes, or until golden brown and crispy.
5. **Serve:**
    - Allow to cool slightly before serving.

These croissants combine the ultimate flavors of spinach and feta in a buttery, flaky pastry. Enjoy!

Ham and Gruyère Croissant

Ingredients:

- 2 large croissants
- 4 oz Gruyère cheese, sliced or shredded
- 4 oz ham, sliced
- 1 tablespoon Dijon mustard (optional)
- 1 tablespoon butter, melted (for brushing)

Instructions:

1. **Prepare the Croissants:**
   - Preheat your oven to 375°F (190°C).
   - Slice the croissants in half lengthwise, but not all the way through.
2. **Assemble the Filling:**
   - If using Dijon mustard, spread it on the inside of each croissant half.
   - Layer the ham and Gruyère cheese inside the croissants.
3. **Bake:**
   - Brush the tops of the croissants with melted butter.
   - Place them on a baking sheet lined with parchment paper.
   - Bake for 10-15 minutes, or until the cheese is melted and the croissants are golden brown.
4. **Serve:**
   - Serve warm for the ultimate crispy and cheesy treat.

This croissant combines the ultimate richness of Gruyère with savory ham, all encased in a flaky pastry. Enjoy!

French Country Ham and Pickle Sandwich

Ingredients:

- 1 baguette or rustic country bread
- 4 oz French country ham or prosciutto, thinly sliced
- 2 tablespoons Dijon mustard
- 1-2 tablespoons mayonnaise
- 4-6 pickles (cornichons or dill pickles), sliced
- 1 small handful of fresh arugula or watercress (optional)
- 1 small red onion, thinly sliced (optional)
- Salt and freshly ground black pepper, to taste

Instructions:

1. **Prepare the Bread:**
   - Slice the baguette or country bread in half lengthwise. If using a baguette, you may want to cut it into sandwich-sized pieces.
2. **Assemble the Sandwich:**
   - Spread Dijon mustard on one side of the bread and mayonnaise on the other side.
   - Layer the ham evenly on one side of the bread.
   - Add pickle slices on top of the ham.
   - Optionally, layer on fresh arugula or watercress and thinly sliced red onion.
3. **Season and Close:**
   - Season with a bit of salt and freshly ground black pepper.
   - Close the sandwich with the other slice of bread.
4. **Serve:**
   - Cut the sandwich into portions if desired and serve immediately.

This sandwich combines the rich flavors of French country ham with the tanginess of pickles, offering a satisfying and rustic meal. Enjoy!

Sweet and Spicy Sausage Baguette
Ingredients:
1 baguette, sliced lengthwise
4 sweet and spicy sausages (such as chorizo or Italian sausage)
1 tablespoon olive oil
1/2 cup caramelized onions
1/4 cup Dijon mustard or spicy brown mustard
1/4 cup mayonnaise (optional)
Fresh parsley or arugula (optional, for garnish)
Instructions:
Cook the Sausages:

Preheat your grill or skillet over medium heat.
Cook the sausages until fully cooked and browned, about 4-5 minutes per side. Slice them into thin rounds.
Prepare the Baguette:

Preheat your oven to 375°F (190°C).
Brush the inside of the baguette slices with olive oil.
Toast them in the oven for about 5-7 minutes, until slightly crispy.
Assemble the Baguette:

Spread mustard and/or mayonnaise on the toasted side of each baguette slice.
Layer the sliced sausages evenly on one side of the baguette.
Top with caramelized onions.
Finish and Serve:

Optionally, garnish with fresh parsley or arugula.
Close the baguette and cut into portions.
This baguette combines the ultimate sweet and spicy flavors with the richness of caramelized onions, creating a delicious and hearty meal. Enjoy!

Eggplant and Mozzarella Sandwich

Ingredients:

- 1 large eggplant, sliced into 1/4-inch rounds
- 2 tablespoons olive oil
- Salt and pepper, to taste
- 4 oz fresh mozzarella, sliced
- 1/4 cup basil pesto or marinara sauce
- 4 slices of crusty bread (like ciabatta or sourdough)
- 1-2 tablespoons balsamic glaze (optional)
- Fresh basil leaves (optional, for garnish)

Instructions:

1. **Prepare the Eggplant:**
   - Preheat your oven to 400°F (200°C).
   - Arrange eggplant slices on a baking sheet. Brush both sides with olive oil and season with salt and pepper.
   - Roast for about 20-25 minutes, flipping halfway through, until tender and slightly browned.
2. **Prepare the Bread:**
   - Toast the bread slices if desired.
3. **Assemble the Sandwich:**
   - Spread basil pesto or marinara sauce on one side of each bread slice.
   - Layer the roasted eggplant slices evenly on two of the bread slices.
   - Top with fresh mozzarella slices.
   - Optionally, drizzle with balsamic glaze and add fresh basil leaves.
4. **Finish and Serve:**
   - Close the sandwiches with the remaining bread slices.
   - Serve immediately, or grill in a panini press or skillet until the cheese is melted and the bread is crispy.

This sandwich combines the rich flavors of roasted eggplant with creamy mozzarella and a touch of pesto or marinara, making for a delightful vegetarian meal. Enjoy!

Chicken and Leek Sandwich

Ingredients:

- 2 cups cooked chicken, shredded or sliced (e.g., roasted or grilled)
- 1 large leek, cleaned and sliced (white and light green parts only)
- 1 tablespoon olive oil
- 2 tablespoons mayonnaise
- 1 tablespoon Dijon mustard
- 4 slices of crusty bread (like sourdough or ciabatta)
- Salt and pepper, to taste
- Fresh herbs (like parsley or thyme), chopped (optional)
- Lettuce or arugula (optional, for added freshness)

Instructions:

1. **Prepare the Leeks:**
    - Heat olive oil in a skillet over medium heat.
    - Sauté the leeks until soft and slightly caramelized, about 5-7 minutes. Season with salt and pepper. Let cool.
2. **Prepare the Chicken Mixture:**
    - In a bowl, mix the cooked chicken with mayonnaise, Dijon mustard, and any fresh herbs if using. Season with salt and pepper.
3. **Assemble the Sandwich:**
    - Spread the chicken mixture evenly on two slices of bread.
    - Top with sautéed leeks.
    - Optionally, add lettuce or arugula for extra crunch.
4. **Finish and Serve:**
    - Top with the remaining bread slices.
    - Serve immediately, or toast in a panini press or skillet for a warm option.

This sandwich brings together the ultimate combination of tender chicken and flavorful leeks, perfect for a hearty and delicious meal. Enjoy!

Grilled Portobello Mushroom Baguette

Ingredients:

- 2 large Portobello mushrooms, cleaned and stems removed
- 2 tablespoons olive oil
- 1 tablespoon balsamic vinegar
- 2 cloves garlic, minced
- Salt and pepper, to taste
- 1 baguette
- 1/4 cup mayonnaise
- 1 tablespoon Dijon mustard
- 1/4 cup fresh basil leaves or arugula
- 1/4 cup grated Parmesan or crumbled feta cheese (optional)

Instructions:

1. **Prepare the Mushrooms:**
   - Preheat your grill or grill pan to medium-high heat.
   - In a bowl, mix olive oil, balsamic vinegar, minced garlic, salt, and pepper.
   - Brush the mixture onto the Portobello mushrooms.
2. **Grill the Mushrooms:**
   - Grill the mushrooms for 4-5 minutes per side, until tender and well-marked. Let cool slightly, then slice.
3. **Prepare the Baguette:**
   - Slice the baguette lengthwise and lightly toast if desired.
4. **Assemble the Sandwich:**
   - Spread mayonnaise and Dijon mustard on the inside of the baguette slices.
   - Layer the grilled mushroom slices on one side of the baguette.
   - Top with fresh basil or arugula, and optionally, grated Parmesan or crumbled feta.
5. **Finish and Serve:**
   - Close the baguette and cut into portions.
   - Serve immediately.

This baguette features the ultimate blend of smoky grilled mushrooms and fresh toppings, making for a deliciously satisfying sandwich. Enjoy!

Pâté and Pickle Baguette

Ingredients:

- 1 baguette
- 4-6 tablespoons pâté (chicken, pork, or your choice)
- 4-6 pickles (cornichons or dill pickles), sliced
- 1 tablespoon Dijon mustard (optional)
- Fresh herbs (like parsley or watercress), for garnish (optional)

Instructions:

1. **Prepare the Baguette:**
   - Slice the baguette lengthwise. You can lightly toast it if you prefer a crispier texture.
2. **Assemble the Sandwich:**
   - Spread a generous layer of pâté on one side of the baguette.
   - Add pickle slices on top of the pâté.
   - Optionally, spread Dijon mustard on the other side of the baguette before closing.
3. **Garnish and Serve:**
   - Garnish with fresh herbs if desired.
   - Close the baguette and cut into portions.

This baguette offers the ultimate combination of rich pâté and tangy pickles, making for a delicious and satisfying sandwich. Enjoy!

Truffle and Mushroom Croissant

Ingredients:

- 2 large croissants
- 1 tablespoon olive oil or butter
- 1 cup mushrooms (such as cremini, shiitake, or button), finely chopped
- 1 clove garlic, minced
- 1 tablespoon truffle oil (or more, to taste)
- 1/4 cup grated Parmesan cheese
- 1 tablespoon fresh thyme leaves (or 1 teaspoon dried thyme)
- Salt and pepper, to taste
- Optional: a few thin slices of fresh truffle (if available) or truffle salt for added flavor

Instructions:

1. **Prepare the Mushrooms:**
    - Heat olive oil or butter in a skillet over medium heat.
    - Add the chopped mushrooms and sauté until they are golden brown and their moisture has evaporated, about 7-10 minutes.
    - Add minced garlic and cook for an additional 1-2 minutes.
    - Stir in truffle oil and thyme. Season with salt and pepper to taste. Remove from heat and let cool slightly.
2. **Prepare the Croissants:**
    - Preheat your oven to 375°F (190°C) if you plan to bake the croissants.
    - If the croissants are not pre-baked, slice them in half lengthwise.
3. **Assemble the Croissant:**
    - Spread the mushroom mixture evenly inside each croissant.
    - Sprinkle grated Parmesan cheese over the mushroom filling.
    - Optionally, add thin slices of fresh truffle or a pinch of truffle salt for extra truffle flavor.
4. **Bake:**
    - Place the assembled croissants on a baking sheet lined with parchment paper.
    - Bake for 5-7 minutes, or until the croissants are warm and the cheese is melted and bubbly.
5. **Serve:**
    - Serve warm and enjoy the rich, earthy flavors of truffle and mushroom in a flaky, buttery croissant.

This croissant combines luxurious truffle with savory mushrooms for a gourmet treat that's perfect for brunch or a special snack. Enjoy!

Mediterranean Veggie Baguette

Ingredients:

- 1 baguette
- 1/4 cup hummus (store-bought or homemade)
- 1/4 cup tzatziki sauce (optional, for extra flavor)
- 1 small cucumber, thinly sliced
- 1 small red bell pepper, thinly sliced
- 1 medium tomato, thinly sliced
- 1/4 cup Kalamata olives, pitted and sliced
- 1/4 cup red onion, thinly sliced
- 1/2 cup crumbled feta cheese
- Fresh basil leaves or arugula (optional, for added freshness)
- Salt and pepper, to taste
- 1 tablespoon olive oil (optional, for drizzling)

Instructions:

1. **Prepare the Baguette:**
     - Slice the baguette lengthwise. You can lightly toast it if you prefer a crispier texture.
2. **Spread the Condiments:**
     - Spread hummus evenly on one side of the baguette. If using tzatziki sauce, spread it on the other side of the baguette.
3. **Layer the Vegetables:**
     - Layer the cucumber slices, red bell pepper slices, and tomato slices evenly on the baguette.
     - Add Kalamata olives and red onion slices on top.
4. **Add Cheese and Garnish:**
     - Sprinkle crumbled feta cheese over the vegetables.
     - Optionally, add fresh basil leaves or arugula for extra flavor and freshness.
5. **Season and Finish:**
     - Season with salt and pepper to taste.
     - Drizzle with olive oil if desired.
6. **Serve:**
     - Close the baguette and cut into portions.
     - Serve immediately, or wrap in parchment paper for a portable lunch.

This baguette brings together a delightful mix of Mediterranean flavors, perfect for a light lunch or a tasty snack. Enjoy!

Warm Goat Cheese and Walnut Tartine

Ingredients:

- 4 slices of rustic bread (such as sourdough or ciabatta)
- 4 oz goat cheese, softened
- 1/4 cup walnuts, roughly chopped
- 2 tablespoons honey
- 1 tablespoon olive oil
- 1-2 tablespoons fresh thyme leaves or rosemary (optional)
- Salt and pepper, to taste
- Fresh arugula or mixed greens (optional, for garnish)

Instructions:

1. **Prepare the Bread:**
    - Preheat your oven to 375°F (190°C).
    - Brush both sides of the bread slices with olive oil.
    - Arrange the bread slices on a baking sheet and toast them in the oven for about 5-7 minutes, or until golden brown and crispy.
2. **Prepare the Goat Cheese:**
    - Spread a generous layer of softened goat cheese on each toasted bread slice.
    - Top with chopped walnuts.
3. **Bake the Tartines:**
    - Return the topped bread slices to the oven and bake for an additional 5-7 minutes, or until the goat cheese is warm and slightly melted.
4. **Finish and Serve:**
    - Drizzle honey over the warm goat cheese and walnuts.
    - Optionally, sprinkle with fresh thyme or rosemary.
    - Season with salt and pepper to taste.
    - Garnish with fresh arugula or mixed greens if desired.
5. **Serve:**
    - Serve the tartines warm.

This tartine offers a delicious combination of creamy goat cheese, crunchy walnuts, and a touch of sweetness from honey, making it a perfect treat. Enjoy!

Roast Beef and Horseradish Sandwich

Ingredients:

- 2 slices of crusty bread (like sourdough or rye)
- 4 oz roast beef, thinly sliced
- 2 tablespoons horseradish sauce (adjust to taste)
- 1 tablespoon mayonnaise
- 1 tablespoon Dijon mustard (optional)
- 1 cup arugula or baby spinach
- 1 small red onion, thinly sliced (optional)
- Salt and pepper, to taste

Instructions:

1. **Prepare the Bread:**
   - Toast the bread slices lightly if desired.
2. **Make the Sauce:**
   - In a small bowl, mix horseradish sauce with mayonnaise. Add Dijon mustard if using. Adjust seasoning with salt and pepper.
3. **Assemble the Sandwich:**
   - Spread the horseradish-mayo mixture evenly on both slices of bread.
   - Layer the roast beef on one slice of bread.
   - Add arugula or baby spinach on top of the roast beef.
   - Optionally, add thinly sliced red onion.
4. **Finish and Serve:**
   - Close the sandwich with the remaining bread slice.
   - Cut in half and serve immediately.

This sandwich combines the ultimate blend of spicy horseradish with tender roast beef for a satisfying and flavorful meal. Enjoy!

Creamy Camembert and Apple Sandwich

Ingredients:

- 2 slices of crusty bread (like sourdough or ciabatta)
- 4 oz Camembert cheese, sliced
- 1 apple (such as Granny Smith or Honeycrisp), thinly sliced
- 1 tablespoon honey
- 1 tablespoon Dijon mustard (optional)
- Fresh arugula or spinach (optional)
- 1 tablespoon butter (for toasting, optional)

Instructions:

1. **Prepare the Bread:**
    - If desired, butter the outside of each bread slice.
    - Toast the bread slices in a skillet or on a griddle over medium heat until golden brown and crispy.
2. **Assemble the Sandwich:**
    - Spread Dijon mustard on one side of each bread slice if using.
    - Layer Camembert cheese evenly on one slice of bread.
    - Arrange apple slices on top of the cheese.
    - Drizzle honey over the apple slices.
    - Add fresh arugula or spinach if desired.
3. **Finish and Serve:**
    - Top with the remaining bread slice.
    - Cut the sandwich in half and serve immediately.

This sandwich offers the ultimate combination of creamy Camembert, crisp apples, and a touch of honey for a delightful contrast of flavors. Enjoy!